The beauty of the way

and the goodness

of the wayfarer

Copyright © 2015 by Roberto Cancel

All rights reserved. This book or any portion thereof may not be reproduced or used in any manner whatsoever without the express written permission of the publisher except for the use of brief quotations in a book review.

First Printing, 2013

Second Edition, 2015

ISBN 978-0-9896767-2-4

The beauty of the way and the goodness of the wayfarer

Musings and moments

from a meandering life

by

Roberto Gil Cancel Comas

To all whose company, smiles, and stories have enriched

my own wanderings.

I'm ever thankful for sharing a path if only for a short time.

Finland

Belgium
Germany

Barcelona   Kosova
Alhambra   Albania Istanbul
           Greece

Morocco

Nepal

China

Thailand

The beauty of the way . . .

Strange Bed

I was made
of something
ephemeral
never meant
to remain
in the same
spot for very long.
Longing for
space that abounds
and confounds
mice and men
in the end
with their plans
and prayers
for stability.

No, not I.
My feet itch
to feel the road
unstrode
while I drift
among the debris
of dreams deferred
by so many
sedentary souls.
By the wind
I am led
in wisps of
aimless meander
on a restless route
to another stop,

a spot on a map
to call home
for today
anyway
and lay
down my head
because when
all is done and said
I sleep better
in a strange bed.

The Map Room

I traveled
the world
in a little
room
in a corner
of the library,
that nobody knows.
I planned trips
to the covers
of National Geographics
and explored
the visions of
map-makers
Mercator even
scoffed at.
My fingers
traced the
parallels,
the meridians,
and contour
lines of infinite
possibility.
I flew over
plastic mountains
painted oceans
and names
I couldn't pronounce
till I found myself
once again
in that little room
not so far
from my house,
but the brick walls
of a library
can never hold the
soul of a nomad
with the heart
of a gypsy
and the feet
of a wayfarer.

This Bit of Road

We have come a long way
And the road is yet long before us
What is behind us is out of sight
What is ahead is still unknown
All we have is this bit of road

So don't strain your eyes on the horizon
Or twist your neck peering back
Because all we have is this here and now
That's all we'll ever have
And more then we could ever ask for

Route 319/98

On my way
to the coast
a road
I know so well
to the demands
of life
I kindly wave
farewell,
for I belong
to only the road
and it
to me
together we move
restlessly to
the sea
to the end
of the world
where all that exists
is sand and surf
and a lost sense
of bliss,
lost in deadlines
and headlines
and frantic ladder climbing,
in traffic horns
and plastic thorns
and wake up calls chiming.

In the sea
there's only me
and the rolling
of the Earth
the softly swaying hips
of the mother
who gave us birth.

Dhermi, Albania

San Blas

En la playa
de mi vida
no existe
final
solo yo, la arena
y la reina
del mar
caminamos
sobre olas
y bailamos
bajo el sol
y nos perdemos
en el aroma
el aroma del amor
no el amor
de uno a la
otra
pero para la vida
simple y
maravillosa
la noche
como el día
está llena
de la luz
de alegría
y la tarde y el alba
no me faltan
de encantar
porque con
mi reina
ningún mal
me puede alcanzar.

Anthong

The singing stillness
of the night
stills my anxious
aching heart
drawn in by
the arching endless
crystalline skies
glitter into oblivion
alive with the flames
of lives and dreams
now only memories
blown upon
the shifting breeze
of the insatiable sea
that bears them
with the foot prints
of forgotten feet
to far off shores
sure to forget
them in time
and sooth
another soul
softly swaying
upon uncertainty
suspended upon
hammock strings
above the sandy floor
as the last grain
of what we
see and seem
slips silently
to sleep.

A Farewell to Sagarmatha

Through the cotton
in my ears
and in the sky
the metallic beast
roared through the air
as it jumped
off the cliff.

We swam in a sea
of fractal marshmallows;
islands of stone and ice
broke the stoic celestial white,
those zebra peaks
so faint and yet familiar
fading into memories.

The mountains ascended
as we descended
to meet the
anxieties of life
but a part of me
would remain
in Sagarmatha
and a part of she
in me.

Cordillera

Crumbs of sun
fell upon
the crumpled bed sheet
mountains
as my last
longing gaze
caressed
the folding fabric
of green leaves
and pine trees
of the home
land
that never fully
belong to me
though I see
it in my mind
like a forgotten mystery
or silent entreaty
to return,
return
where?

A Gypsy's Song

I dream
of a place
undiscovered and new
and toss and turn in bed
wishing it were true.
So I tie my shoes
and I say goodbye.
Slowly I make my way
up the mountain side.
The trail is hard
and the trail is long
but quiet steadily
I walk on.

The peaks
touch the sky,
I'm dressed in clouds
as I heave a hearty sigh.
I see the sea
spread out below,
at what distance
I don't rightfully know.
But I look down
and cinch my coat;
I leave the cold
and I clear my throat.
To the beat of my boots
I compose a song
to keep me company
as I walk on.

Guilin, China

My feet sink
in the sand;
I think I've finally reached
the end of the land.
Then a boatman
glides toward me;
Where you going,
his silent inquiry.
'to the other side,'
I quickly lied,
pretending to know
what the sea has in store.
I turned to watch
the disappearing shore,
as it's claimed
by another fiery dawn.
Pacing the deck,
I walk on.

I reach a city,
sprawling and wide;
there's life and entertainment
to every side.
Lost in its streets
beautiful things I found,
as my soles
slowly wore down.
Drunk on burlesque,
I found the wharf
and there's the boatman,
just like before.
In his eyes
I see my reply,
'it's time to go home,
I've gone too long.'
I mount the plank,
and I walk on.

I step onto a familiar shore,
every tree, every stone
I've seen before.
My friends greet me
with joy and love;
they shower hugs and kisses
like rain from above.
I try to return their affection
as best as I can,
but I am overwhelmed;
I'm only one man.
Everything is safe
calm and full of peace.
Everything that is to say
except - me.
So I raise my glass
to quell the happy song,
'I love you all dearly,
but I must walk on.'

To my surprise
no one's angry or sad,
they hug me like before;
their love is no fad.
They pack my bag
and make me food.
They kiss my forehead
and bid me adieu.
There are tears in my eyes
as I wave goodbye,
but joy in my heart
as I face the dawn.
Carrying their love,
I walk on.

Fez, Morocco

Inquieto

Amar y ser amado
tranquilo y reposado
en tus brazos esperando
la noche de encanto
la luz bajita en tu carita
con ojos que suave gritan
'Has llegado a mi lado
y que nunca seas apartado.'
¿Qué más puedo yo pedir?
¿Qué más puedo yo decir
cuando en silencio me inquieto
y de pronto yo me muevo,
cuando mi bulto está empacado
y tu mirada ha cambiado?
¿Qué más puedo yo decir
sin tu corazón herir?
Te amo y te amaré
pero hoy te dejaré,
no por buscar otro querer
sino buscar mi propio ser,
andando muchos caminos
hasta caer en mi destino,
y a esa fuerza yo le pido
que un día andes conmigo.

Donde Quiera

Donde quiera
que ando,
oigo tu risa
en el soplar
de la briza.

Donde quiera
que ando,
veo tu mirada
en las nubes
nevadas.

Donde quiera
que ando,
siento tu calor
en cada rayo
del sol.

Donde quiera
que ando,
palpita tu corazón
en mis pasos
y respiración.

Donde quiera
que ando,
tú sigues conmigo
es lo único
que te pido.

The Promise

From our first gasp of breath
to our last heavy sigh
our time seems to pass
in a blink of god's eye.

Let him blink us away
like so many salty tears
as we pass from this life
full of dread and fear.

Whatever may come next,
if anything at all,
let us enjoy what we have;
let us revel in our fall.

We are fickle and we fail
when life needs us most,
when we are called to be strong
we give up the ghost.

We hurt the ones we love
and we love far too few,
and forgiveness is rare
when giving others their due.

But in spite of our faults
and all our mortal sins,
or perhaps because of them,
we are capable of beautiful things.

Every breath is a miracle,
every tear is divine,
every ache, every pain,
is another sign we are alive.

Turku, Finland

Every beat of a broken heart
gives us hope we'll love again
and again be hurt and hurt
in a cycle without end.

But a cycle full of love
a cycle full of hope,
a hope against all odds,
a love beyond our scope.

It's something we can't understand
something we cannot know
and not knowing gives us faith
not knowing makes us grow.

It makes us open to the world
and the twisted path we walk
making us forget the brutalities
upon us life has wrought.

And every act of kindness
done for a stranger or a friend
helps to remind us that
we're all connected in the end.

A sea of souls crashing
from shore to shore
rolling over each other
in a ceaseless uproar.

We bump and we jostle,
we punch and we claw,
but sometimes we reach out
and help another move on.

And that ripple of good
moves through us all
and moves us all closer
to the promise before the fall.

. . . the goodness of the wayfarer.

'Es tan corto el amor...'

'I love you's
are always
written in sand,
smoky breath
on a winter's day,
the things we say
exist ephemeral
only in the present
tense, tension with
the unknowable future.

Today,
the only day
emotions know
can know,
can't escape,
rules lovers
like an enlightened despot
desperate
to carpe diem,
seizing himself
in seizures of
ecstasy.

'I love you's
bloom and wilt
like the blush
rouge roses
they accompany,
lovelier for the loss
they portend;
silk a flower
will never make
nor a ring a lover.
So strew your petals
upon the beach
and watch
the waves come in
for they'll never
look lovelier
then in the
letting go
as is your
longing heart so.

Your laugh

Your laugh
like an inner child
too tickled
with body still
in giddy thrill
I kiss your
teeth
your smile
never ends
your laugh
never ends
and I am silent
not to miss
one gasping moment
of heartfelt hilarity
my heart and breath
thud and hiss
and hiss and thud
in time with
your chest
your laugh
with disregard
with the passion
of a heretic
and the bliss
of a believer
moves me
your laugh
like no one's around
for everyone to hear
your heedless
wholesome
holy laugh.

So Lovely

You – are – so – lovely
inside and out
from top to bottom
from the side and
from in between –
I love your loveliness
that loves me
just like this
as I am
no judgments,
no demands;
I love the beat
of your heart
against mine
racing in time
in the most
divine rhyme
creation ever
created.

The Light of your Eyes

With city stars
at our feet
and aurora
in your eyes,
we sat in such peace
that knew no compromise.
I listened
to your words
and got lost
in the sound.
I wondered
at their beauty
and the beauty
I had found.
I wondered
how to keep it
without holding
too tight
without wanting
too much
without losing sight
of the fragility
of the moment
that made it
so pure
ensuring that
in my memory
it would always
endure.
And so . . .
I learned
to keep it
by letting go
by letting it
wash over me
by letting it
flow
from one second
to the next
and to the next
unknown
knowing only
that eventually
the moment
would be gone
and you . . .
with it
left only
a memory
but one so perfect
of perfect sincerity
like a prism
of life
so brilliant
and rare
rending
asunder
all our hopes
and despair
making a rainbow
of dreams,
of fantasy and
surprise
constantly shifting
like the light
in your eyes.

Morocco

You made

You made me
forget I was shy
and a-fraid
knot of heart strings
bound so tight
that barely a beat
could beat its way out
I forgot about
the game
I never knew
how to play
and that I
didn't want
to play it anyway
you made
everything clear
like a memory
of another life
I lived before
I was born
or torn
from my mother's womb
the way you know
water quenches thirst
and before you
can walk
you must crawl first
I knew your face
in a place
in me
that words
do not describe
and I thank you
for being there
and being here
and making in me
a luck that
could never be
or I could never see
without you
here.

Vesanca, Finland

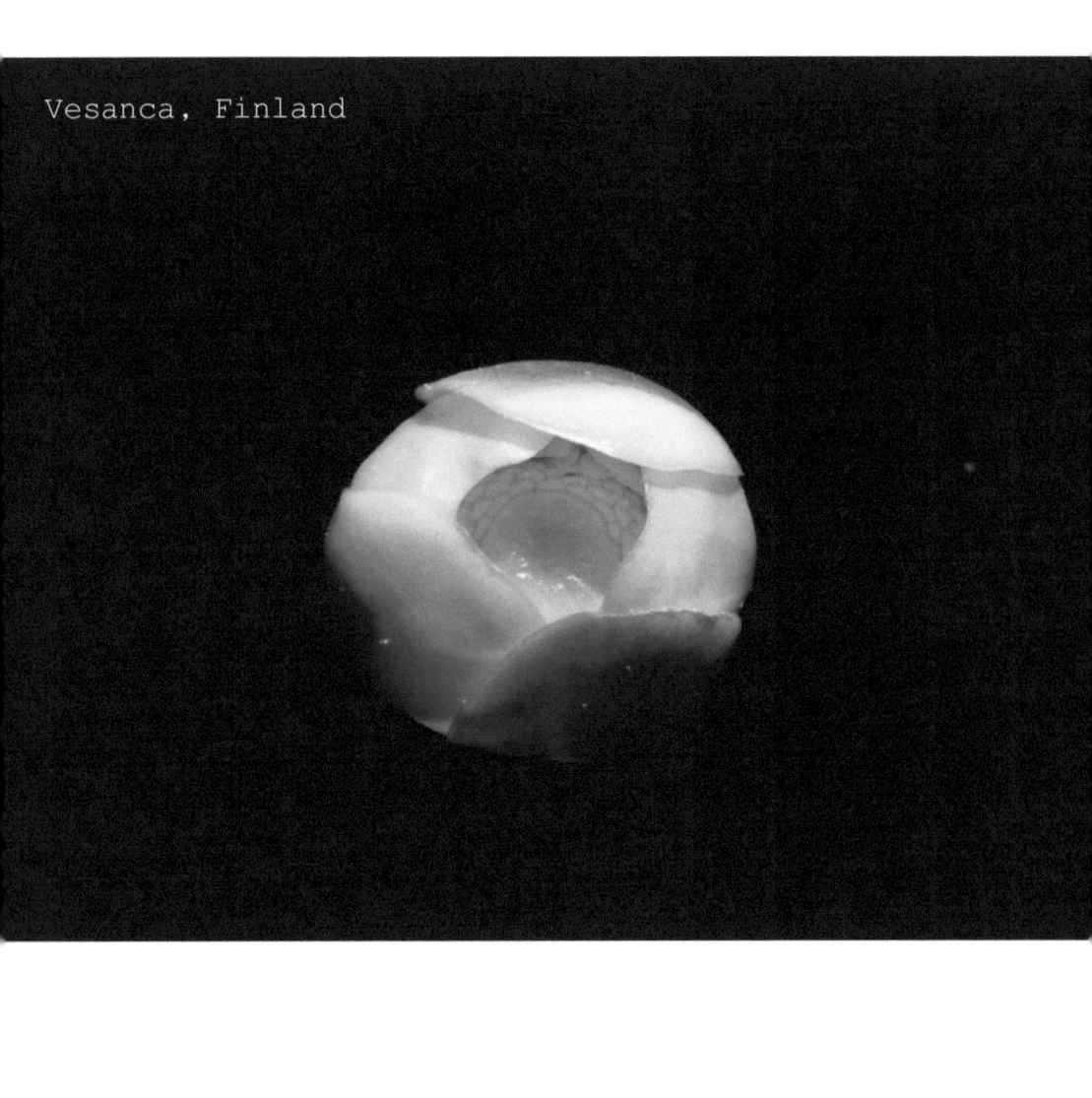

Singularity

In the thrust
of passion,
we rub
and the dust
and sweat
of our bodies join
in the slipperiness
that fills the
dimensions
between us;
we slide over
each other in
the union of
our essences.
Where do I end?
In extension
through you
I am infinite.
In one
undulating form
we encompass
the universe
joined in the most
complete singularity,
but like all things
since the big bang
we must move apart;
our celestial bodies
descend in exhaustion.
Slowly we peel
ourselves apart
like a cell
in mitosis,
but who knows
how much of me
is in you
and you
in me,
still one
singularity,
in two
vessels.

Barcelona

A Kinda Crazy

I'm crazy
for the want
of you
I haven't lost
my mind
instead I've
lost my time,
hours full of
thoughts of
things abstract
have lost ground
to something
more
intact
memories and
prophesies
of the beauty
that has been
and could be
between us.
I close my
eyes and
the elegant universe
dissolves
into numbness
numbers
while your face
comes shining
through the
light years and
the millennia
and fills
my view
with something
new and fresh,
and unbelievable,
because the logic
that governs apples
languishes
in the hearts
of lovers
and love
becomes derivative
in the scope
of calculus.
So let my thoughts
and hours
and minutes
be lost
if in that
losing
a second
becomes
an eternity
with you.

Far from Istanbul

How far we've come
from the wordless wonder
of one of our first nights
together,
watching the sunset
over a city
so foreign yet familiar
basking in the beauty
of a moment
fated to end
in darkness.

How our lives have changed
through intimacy
and distance,
growing together,
then apart;
like the restless sea
seeking the shore
but always retreating
from its embrace.

Like the sun
and the sea
you are gone
but forever with me
imprinted
on my mind
and my shifting heart.

As I depart,
to that same city
on the sea,
I know I am better
than I would be
without having
loved you.

Me Despierto

Me despierto
pensando en ti
y pienso
en despertarme
contigo.

Pienso
en la luminosa fragancia
del amanecer
y de tu piel
envuelta
en una sabana
de inocencia
y silencio.

Beso tus ojos
durmientes
y en tu oído respiro
'Te amo,'
pero cuando mis caricias
te despiertan
como un sueño
tu imagen
se deshace
y yo me quedo solo
con el silencio.

For Want of a Crescent Moon

I miss
your smile
my dear
I miss
that glow
that pictures
can't show
I miss
you being
here
I miss
the ecstatic
bubbling babbling
excitement of
your presence
your essence
that I long
to capture
in an embrace
I want
to squeeze you
till the line
between us
bends
to the pressure
of pleasure
and I lose
your face
in mine
I miss
the sweet
things said
in whispers
so slight
that memory
catches only
the essence
of a mood
in a moment
ineffable
but unforgettable
I miss
all this
and so much
more
but all these
words I use
to say I miss
pale in comparison
to just one kiss.

A Room for Me

There was something about that room that was more home than mine; that room a womb of warmth and affectionate whispers swapped under cozy sheets, misty day light that slipped through the slight curtains of your design, and the universe swaying softly above us for us only. Perhaps it was your aroma in the air even when you weren't there, but I felt loved between those walls. Through the hours of ecstasy and bliss and even when things were amiss, I knew this: there was room for me there. When the world was whirling too fast to take notice of me there was room for me there, between the planets and the plants, between the cranes and the kiddos, between the photos and the phantoms of years yellowed with time there was room for me in your room and in your heart.

Half Sublime

You call me
from a speeding car
so far
away
it is a whisper
upon the roar
of six cylinders.
I love you
because
I don't know you;
I lost you
because
I don't care.
The thrill
of the unreal
I steal
and nothing more.
I like the shadow
upon the wall,
the light
of truth
gives me
only bricks,
and sticks
that break
the bones of
uncertainty,
mystery,
divinity.
But the morning
will come
and the bar stools
will reach for
the rising sun
and forget
the silhouettes
that passed
between them.
It's just
a finger up
my spine
only half sublime;
a caterpillar
in my gut
that never
learned how
to fly.

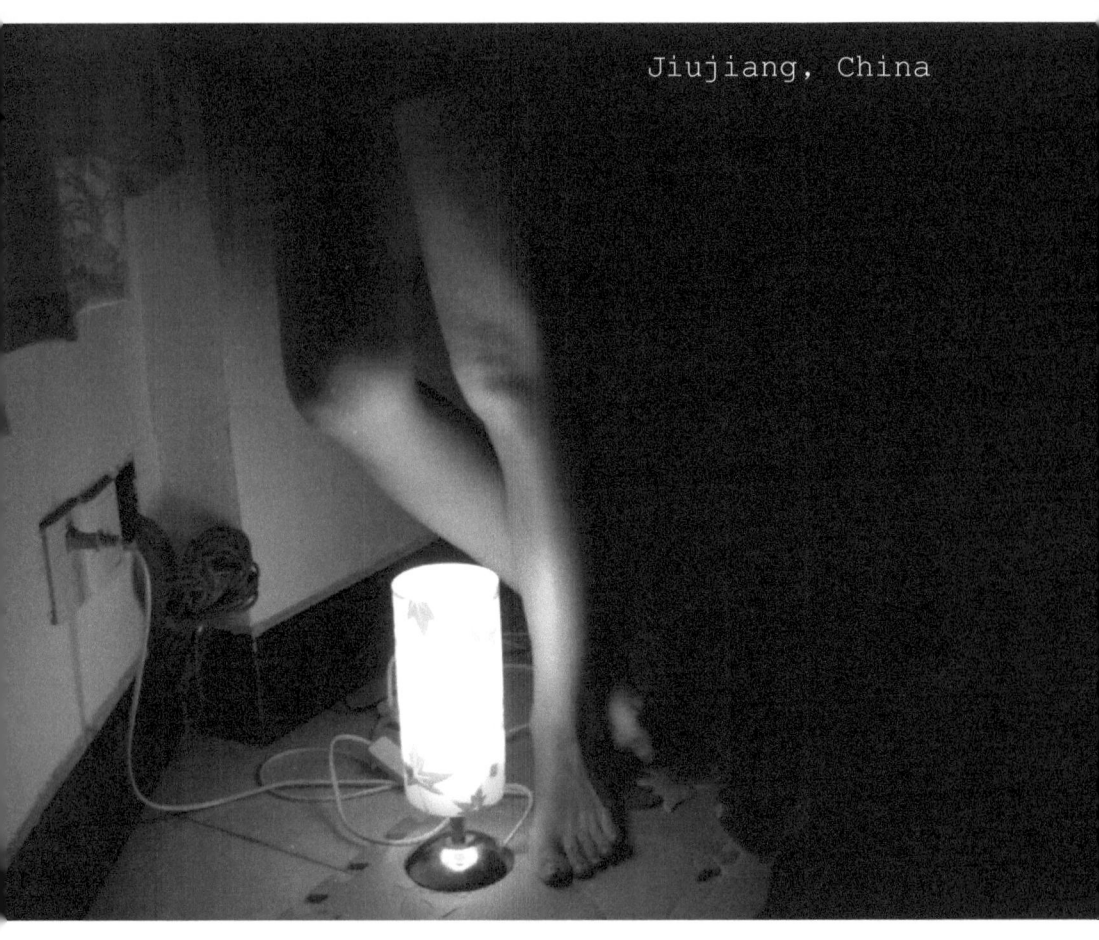

The Same Stranger

I wake to find
the same stranger
in my bed again
I know her
well enough
to kiss and miss
her presence
when I'm gone
but her intentions
and pretensions
are still a mystery
to me.
Her touch
is warm,
warm enough
to melt my flesh
and guarded apathy,
but her words
and shoulder
are cold still
and chill
the marrow
of my longing.
Like a jester
learning to joggle
first with torches
instead of rubber balls
all I can do
is hold on tight
when and where
the flame doesn't fall
knowing well,
as I always knew,
I'll be burned
before the jest
is through.

New Love, New Horizon

With you
everything feels new
like a morning sky
of the deepest blue
high and arching
without a cloud in sight
an empty void
of the darkest bright
yet filled
and filling me
with all the beauty
of what could be
and the nimbus clouds
around
my heart and mind
are dispersed
by your words so kind
and with them
all my anxiety and fear
my uncertain longing
which I held so dear
are cleared
from my consciousness
like an early fog
releasing my heart
from its frozen gulag
I love you
and your love
is not wanting
it is blissfully complete
and free of all taunting
self-doubt and critique
which torture
my wary soul
no, with you
I am safe
and my horizon
is whole.

Secret Song

A secret song
resides in my heart
like a ballerina-ed
music box
who's lid
knows only
the tender touch
of your sincerest soul
full of the seeds
of dreams
sown in the
brilliant tapestry
of your affection
and imagination
your expressions
of self
sing my song
into me
and let
me see
the world
for the work
of art
in progress
it could
and should be
as I see it
in your eyes.

Entrego

Te entrego
mi mapa
y zapatos errantes,
y te pido
que me lleves
adonde te place.

Porque en
mis viajes
he comprendido
que mi alma
es un pájaro
y tu corazón
es su nido.

Y todos mis deseos
se encuentran
sometidos
cuando tus
suaves palabras
encuentran mi oído.

Pues no me dejes
vagando
sin dirección ni guía
porque solo
en tu presencia
existe mi alegría.

I hand over
my map
and my arrant shoes
and ask that
you take me
wherever you choose.

Because in
my travels
I have found
my soul
is a bird
and to your
heart it's bound.

And all my desires
are lost
or disappear
when your
sweet words
reach my ear.

So don't leave me
wandering
lost without a guide
because only
in your presence
does my happiness reside.

我交给你
我的地图
和旅游鞋
和请求你
随便带我
因为在旅时
我明白过
我的心灵
是一只鸟
和你的心
是它的巢
和我听你
柔话的时
我的希望
都消失
请不让我
还游荡
无某种导
也无方向
因为仅仅
我附近你
我的幸运
还可以

Index

A Gypsy's Song	17
A Farewell to Sagarmatha	13
A Kinda Crazy	45
A Room for Me	53
Anthong	11
Cordillera	15
Donde Quiera	25
'Es tan corto el amor …'	33
Entrego	63
Far from Istanbul	47
For Want of a Crescent Moon	51
Half Sublime	55
Inquieto	23
Me Despierto	49
New Love, New Horizon	59
Route 319/98	7
San Blas	9
Secret Song	61
Singularity	43

Strange Bed	...	...	...	1
So Lovely	...	...	...	37
The Light of your Eyes	...	...	...	39
The Map Room	...	...	...	3
The Promise	...	...	...	27
The Same Stranger	...	...	...	57
This Bit of Road	...	...	...	5
Your Laugh	...	...	...	35
You made	...	...	...	41

About the Author

Roberto Gil Cancel Comas, was made in Tallahassee, Florida with parts from Puerto Rico. He was the youngest child of his family and grew up with the freedom and understanding from his parents that is unique to that situation.

An anthropologist by training, a development worker by profession, and a wanderer in practice, Roberto has lived on four different continents and travelled through many beautiful countries and the lives of many wonderful people.

Roberto has written since he learned how, for his own amusement and peace of mind. Through these writings, he hopes to share some of the beauty he has witnessed in his meandering search for the meaning of 'home.'

www.ingramcontent.com/pod-product-compliance
Lightning Source LLC
Chambersburg PA
CBHW040440190426
43202CB00033B/6